COWBOYS AND THE WILD WEST

Hilarie N. Staton

KINGFISHER

NEW YORK

All About America: COWBOYS AND THE WILD WEST
All rights reserved. No part of this book may be reproduced or utilized in any form or by any means, electronic or mechanical, including photocopying, recording, or by any information storage or retrieval systems, without permission in writing from the publisher.

KINGFISHER
LONDON & NEW YORK

Published in the United States by Kingfisher,
175 Fifth Ave., New York, NY 10010
Kingfisher is an imprint of Macmillan Children's Books, London.
All rights reserved.

Distributed in the U.S. by Macmillan, 175 Fifth Ave.,
New York, NY 10010
Distributed in Canada by H.B. Fenn and Company Ltd.,
34 Nixon Road, Bolton, Ontario L7E 1W2

Library of Congress Cataloging-in-Publication data has been applied for.

ISBN paperback 978-0-7534-6510-3
ISBN reinforced library binding 978-0-7534-6582-0

Kingfisher books are available for special promotions and premiums. For details contact: Special Markets Department, Macmillan, 175 Fifth Ave., New York, NY 10010.

For more information, please visit www.kingfisherbooks.com

Printed in China
10 9 8 7 6 5 4 3 2 1
1TR/0311/WKT/UNTD/140MA

The All About America series was produced for Kingfisher by Bender Richardson White, Uxbridge, U.K.
Editor: Lionel Bender
Designer: Ben White
DTP: Neil Sutton
Production: Kim Richardson
Consultant: Richard Jensen, Research Professor of History, Culver Stockton College, Missouri

Sources of quotations and excerpts

Pages 5, 10, 11, 15, 21, 26, 28: interview quotes in Library of Congress: American Life Histories: Manuscripts from the Federal Writer's Project, 1936–1940.
Page 8: Ranching profits quote: Thayer, William Makepeace. *Marvels of the New West*, p. 547. Norwich, CT: The Henry Bill Publishing Company, 1890.
Page 12: W. H. Thomas Quote: Slatta, Richard W. *Cowboy: The Illustrated History*, p. 19. Sterling, 2006.
Pages 16, 18: song lyrics in *Cowboy Songs and Other Frontier Ballads*, p. 10. Collected by John A. Lomax and Alan Lomax. NY: The Macmillan Company, 1938.
Page 19: stampede and rustlers quotes: Abbott, E. C. "Teddy Blue" and Helena Huntington Smith. *We Pointed Them North, Recollections of a Cowpuncher*, pp. 66, 70. Chicago, IL: R. R. Donnelley & Sons Company, 1991.
Page 23: Dubbs: Dodge City quote: Goodnight, Charles, Emanuel Dubbs, John A. Hart, and others. *Pioneer Days in the Southwest, From 1850–1879*, p. 35. Guthrie, OK: The State Capital Company, 1909.
Page 24: Wild Bill Hickok quote: Harger, Charles Moreau. "Cattle Trails of the Prairie." *Scribner's Magazine*, volume 11, issue 6, June, 1892.
Page 25: Elfego Baca quote: Smith, Janet. Interview with Elfego Baca, p.1. New Mexico: July 13, 1936.

Acknowledgments

The publishers would like to thank the following illustrators for their contribution to this book: Richard Berridge, Christian Hook, and John James. Map: Neil Sutton. Book cover design: Michael Yuen.
Cover artwork: John James.
The publishers thank the following for supplying photos for this book: b = bottom, c = center, l = left, t = top, m = middle: © The Art Archive: pages 18t (The Art Archive/Bill Manns) • © The Bridgeman Art Library: Peter Newark Western Americana pages 8t, 18m; 13t (Hogg Brothers Collection, Gift of Miss Ima Hogg); 17t (Christie's Images); 26bl (Peter Newark American Pictures); 26 (Peter Newark Pictures); 28l (Peter Newark American Pictures) • © Dorling Kindersley: pages 6t (Geoff Brightling); 19 (Frank Greenaway); 20t and cover (Geoff Brightling) • © istockphoto.com: pages 8–9b (Dale Reardon); 10ml (Manuel Velasco); 10bl (Stanley Lange); 16t (DNY59); 19t (Robert Kohlhuber); 22tl (Don Nichols); 23tl (Renee Lee); 26–27 (Vladimir Maravic); 28tl (Milos Luzanin); 29mr (Kriss Russell) • © Library of Congress: pages 1c and cover (LC-DIG-ppmsca-17869); 1, 2–3, 30–31, 32 (LC-DIG-ppmsc-02629); 4b (LC-DIG-ppmsca-08795); 7tl (LC-DIG-pga-03118); 8–9m (LC-DIG-pga-01454); 10t (LC-DIG-ppmsca-17998); 10b (LC-DIG-ppmsc-02632); 12–13 (LC-DIG-ppmsca-08791); 15b (LC-USZ62-56646); 16 (LC-DIG-ppmsc-02638); 29tl (LC-USZC4-8945); 29ml (LC-USZC4-2740) • © Sears Roebuck: page 27r • © www.shutterstock.com: pages 12tl (Sascha Burkard); 12–13 (Olivier Le Queinec); 14t (Mike Flippo); 22m (CreativeHQ); 22bl (CreativeHQ); 23tr and cover (CreativeHQ); 22tr (J. Helgason); 22hr (Bryan Sikora) • © TopFoto.co.uk: Topham Picturepoint page 4; The Granger Collection/TopFoto pages 5, 6tr, 7tl, 6–7, 7bl, 7mr, 8bl, 8bm, 9tl, 14–15, 15t, 16bl, 18b, 20m, 21t, 21m, 22bm and cover, 23–23, 25, 29bl; World History Archive/TopFoto page 23m.
Every effort has been made to trace the copyright holders of the images. The publishers apologize for any omissions.

CONTENTS

Introduction

Cowboys and the Wild West looks at an exciting part of everyday life in America from the early 1800s to around 1890. It focuses on how Spanish pioneers brought cattle from Mexico to Texas and set up ranches. Other pioneers built ranches, too. The men who took care of the cattle and horses were cowboys. The story is presented as a series of double-page articles, each one looking at a particular topic, including how cowboys worked, lived, enjoyed themselves—and got into trouble. It is illustrated with paintings, engravings, and photographs from the time, mixed with artists' impressions of everyday scenes and situations.

Cowboy Country

Cattle roaming wild and then moved to market

The story of cowboys and western ranches is one of the open range, panicky cattle, horse-riding skills, and railroads. It is about the trip cowboys and cattle took together over long, dangerous trails and the legacies that cowboys have left us.

Before Spanish settlers arrived, much of Texas was empty grassland area. Where the weather was mostly dry, the grass was short and scrubby. In wetter areas, the grass was tall and lush, and streams and rivers cut across the flat prairie and rolling hills. Grasslands reached all the way north into Canada, and the main grazing animal was the mighty buffalo. This land turned out to be perfect for grazing cattle.

Clearing the Plains of Buffalo

Vast herds of buffalo, or American bison, covered the plains until the 1870s. Then these huge animals were hunted for their skins, which were used for blankets and leather clothing and to make belts for machines. By the mid-1880s, the buffalo were gone from the range.

Getting cattle to market for profit

In 1521, the Spanish brought a few cattle to Texas. Ranchers let their cattle run free on Texas's open range. These cattle became the Texas longhorns, which survived and thrived. Cowboys gathered the ranchers' herds only when they needed to use them. Yet there were more cattle than the people nearby needed for meat, hides, or tallow. When the railroads came to the plains in the 1870s, ranchers realized they could ship their cattle to stockyards and slaughter houses in big cities and make a profit. They just had to round up the cattle and get them to the railroads.

▶ Cowboys spent most of their time with the cattle. The main breed of cattle, the Texas longhorn, had huge horns, was stubborn, and got scared easily but could survive for days without water.

▲ Cattle included the young (calves and heifers), adult females (cows), adult males for mating (bulls), and other adult males (steers).

◀ This map shows the cattle trails from Texas's open range to the railroads, hundreds of miles north. Leading the cattle along a trail was a dangerous trip, but once the cattle were loaded into railroad cars, the cowboys celebrated.

CANADA

N

Kansas City

Abilene

Sedalia

St. Louis

Dodge City

GOODNIGHT – LOVING TRAIL

WESTERN TRAIL

CHISHOLM TRAIL

OLD SHAWNEE TRAIL

MEXICO

San Antonio

Texas Cattle

The cattle brought by the Spanish settlers adapted and produced the Texas longhorn. After 1850, Texas ranchers brought shorthorns and brown-and-white Herefords from England, and the all-white Brahman from India. Ranchers mixed these breeds to develop healthy, fast-growing cattle that provided good meat.

Longhorn

Brahman

Shorthorn

Hereford

The golden era of the cowboy

During the main cowboy period, from 1867 until the 1880s, cattle drives went from Texas to railroad towns in Kansas. Being on a drive involved hard, dirty, lonely, and low-paid work, and there were dangers from cattle stampedes and outlaws. Work on a ranch was only a little easier. Sometimes after being on the range or trail, cowboys might celebrate too much, but most had a strong code of honor. The era ended when settlers fenced in the land, railroads expanded, and years of storms killed cattle. Today, cowboys are still working with cattle, using many of the same methods.

As the drives ended, writers and showmen told stories about cowboy life. The stories and movies made about them pictured an exciting life for cowboys, lawmen, rustlers, and outlaws. However, L. M. Cox, a real cowboy, said, "The cowboy's life as we know it was certainly lacking in the glamour which we see on our screens today."

Opening New Markets

In May 1869, railroads from the East and West coasts joined. The new railroads provided a way for ranchers to get their cattle to profitable big city markets. First, though, thousands of cattle from Texas's open range had to be moved to the railroads.

Vaqueros

Skilled horsemen from Mexico

Christopher Columbus brought horses and cattle to the Americas. Later, *vaqueros* used techniques from Spain to care for the cattle, and settlers learned these skills from them.

▲ A cowboy's leather *tapaderas*, or stirrup covers, to protect his feet from the weather

Soldiers, missionaries, and settlers from Spain brought live animals with them on their ships. In Mexico, some cattle and horses escaped and formed wild herds. The animals were free to anyone who could catch and manage them. Some of the Spanish settlers became very skilled at riding horses and roping cattle. These men became known as *vaqueros*, which is a Spanish word for cowboys. On farms, or ranches, they helped raise the cattle, which were used for meat, hides, and tallow. Hides are tanned animal skins that are made into leather for clothes, boots, saddles, and harnesses. Tallow is fat that is boiled down and used to make soap and candles. Ranches sold their cattle, often to the missions or to feed soldiers.

▼ The escaped Spanish cattle roamed free in Texas and slowly adapted to the local conditions. Within a few generations, they had formed a new breed, the Texas longhorns.

▲ *Vaqueros* adapted Spanish skills and equipment to work with cattle in the Americas. This *vaquero*'s saddle, spurs, lariat, and leather chaps were similar to those that were used in Spain.

Vaqueros and other cowboys rode the range, rounded up wild cattle, and branded them.

Fancy but Practical

Vaqueros wore fancy clothes that were just as practical as the working clothes of later cowboys. The wide brim of the *vaquero*'s sombrero and the cowboy's hat kept off the sun and rain. The tall boots and leather chaps protected their legs from horse bites and cacti.

Early ranches and trail drives

In the 1830s, many U.S. citizens moved west to Texas, set up ranches, and learned cowboy skills from the *vaqueros* who were already working there. Nearby, in what is now Oklahoma, American Indians raised cattle, too. They had been forced by the government to move to this area, called Indian Territory. Some had been allowed to bring their cattle, and they became skilled cowboys.

Over the following years, the number of cattle grew. Ranchers hired cowboys to round up their cattle, and some sent small herds to New Orleans or the Texas Gulf Coast to breed on ranches there or to be shipped to other places. In 1846, the first long cattle drive went from Texas to Ohio. The drive was hard on the animals and cowboys. The cattle lost weight and were very thin when they arrived. Then, in 1861, the Civil War began. Texas joined the South, and many cowboys left to enlist in the Confederate army. At first cattle were sent to feed Confederate soldiers, but then the Union army blocked the Mississippi River, so the cattle could not reach the Confederates. Without *vaqueros* and other cowboys to care for them, the cattle were left alone on the open range.

▶ In California, American Indians were trained to be *vaqueros* for the Spanish missions.

Catching Mustangs

When Spanish horses escaped, they formed wild herds. These horses were called mustangs. Mustangs were prized by both American Indians, such as the Comanche, and cowboys. Riders valued the endurance and speed of these small horses. But some could not be tamed.

The Cattle Business

Getting rich by feeding the nation

An 1890 book, *Marvels of the New West*, states: "The profits of stock-raising are marvelous. For this reason, men endure hardships and brave dangers, dwelling apart from friends and civilized society."

Ranchers returned to Texas after the Civil War to find their ranches falling apart. Some six million cattle were running wild on the Texas range, but there was no place nearby to sell them. In 1866, Charles Goodnight rounded up around 2,000 head of cattle and traveled west to New Mexico and Colorado. He sold his cattle at a big profit. The next year, Joseph McCoy built a stockyard near the Abilene, Kansas, railroad station. He encouraged ranchers to bring their cattle to his stockyard, where buyers bought the cattle and shipped them east by rail. At first, companies shipped live cattle to the East. Then, using new technology, the meatpacking industry shipped fresh meat, canned meat, and other products.

Cattle Barons

The men who owned the biggest ranches, had the most power, and made the most money were called cattle barons. Those pictured above started as cowboys, saved all their money, and bought cattle and land until they owned a large ranch. However, Charles Lux began as a California butcher before becoming a cattleman. Before he became president, Teddy Roosevelt invested in a cattle ranch and learned to do a cowboy's job. Other investors only stood and watched cowboys working.

▼ The hard work of raising cattle was done by cowboys.

8

◀ African American Arther Walker became a cowboy when he was 15 years old.

The ranching business changes

By the 1870s, the beef-hungry markets of the Northeast were making increasing demands on the cattle-rich ranges of the Southwest. Ranchers needed money to expand. Some ranchers created companies and sold shares in them to rich investors in New York and foreign countries—such as Scotland and England. A number of foreign investors had a rancher, such as Charles Goodnight, as a partner. Others hired a foreign manager who may never have seen an American ranch.

Ranches expanded, and most ran their cattle on thousands of acres of public land. It was not unusual for ranchers to fence off huge sections of it, including watering holes, for their private use. The largest cattle companies had several ranches. On a Texas ranch, a company might have tried to breed better cattle, while on a ranch in northern states such as Wyoming, they fattened up cattle before they were sold.

Poorly Paid Cowboys
Many former African-American slaves, as well as Mexicans and American Indians, became cowboys. They worked just as hard as white cowboys but often got paid less.

▼ Ranchers bred longhorns with other breeds, such as Scottish shorthorn cattle. The new breeds were not as nervous as Texas longhorns.

◀ Live animals were sent by rail to slaughter houses, where they were killed and their meat sold to butchers.

◀ A cowboy jingled when he walked because of the chains that helped hold his spurs on to his boots.

On the Ranch
Work to be done all year round

On a ranch, everyone had jobs to do to keep the place running smoothly. The rancher, his family, and his cowboys were always busy and worked hard.

The biggest ranches, or outfits, employed more than 150 cowboys. Cowboys fixed equipment, built corrals, and trained horses. They even gathered dry cow chips (cow manure) to burn, as many ranches did not have enough wood nearby to keep cooking and heating fires going. Cowboys often rode out to make sure the cattle were healthy and not hurt. They also checked the windmills to keep them pumping water so the cattle could drink.

In the winter, some cowboys left the ranch because there was not enough work for everyone. Others stayed to make or fix equipment such as branding irons, horse harnesses, and the chuck wagon. Still other cowboys spent long, lonely months in freezing cabins on the range. They rode around to check on the cattle. In really cold weather, they broke through the ice on ponds and water troughs so the cattle could drink.

◀ These are branding irons. Every ranch registered its own brand, which was a unique letter group, number, or picture.

Spring Round-up

During a round-up, cowboys from several ranches brought in the cattle from the open range. They separated the cattle so each ranch had only those that wore its brand. Each outfit branded its new calves and identified the steers it would take on the cattle drive. L. M. Cox, a rancher in the 1880s, said they "were off before daylight and rode hard until after dark . . . [They'd] round up together around 10 o'clock then work cattle or brand until dark and oftentimes stand guard one-third of the night after that."

▼ Several cowboys held down a calf while one branded it. He heated the branding iron in a fire and then pressed it into the side of the calf.

Women ranchers

Few women lived on ranches, so cowboys were protective of the rancher's wife and daughters. Women might run a ranch because their husbands had died, or because they had taken over the family business. In 1886, Mabel Luke married rancher Jim Madison. "I liked ranch life right from the start, for I rode the range with Jim, learned to cook and eat chuck wagon food and to ride and rope with the best of them. Our cowpunchers were a jolly bunch and always ready for a good time. We got lots of fun out of rodeos, chuck suppers, roping contests and dances. Our ranch was the J-M ranch, and our cattle was branded with the J on the shoulder, the bar on the side, and the M on the hip."

Bunkhouse Living

At the ranch, cowboys lived in the bunkhouse. Each had a bed to call his own and a place for his belongings. The cowboys decorated the walls with pictures of loved ones or pictures from magazines or catalogs. But in the summer, the cowboys would sleep outside to escape the bugs, heat, and smells that came from sweaty men.

▶ A ranch might have a wooden house, a barn, a bunkhouse, a cookhouse, and many corrals.

◀ Ranchers hired bronco-busters—cowboys who specialized in training wild horses. They tamed, or busted, these broncos so others could ride them.

In the Saddle
On horseback daybreak to nightfall

Most cowboys did not own much, but everything they had helped them do their job. Their work was usually done while riding horseback, roping, and caring for the cattle and horses.

A cowboy's hat kept off the sun, rain, and dust. He used it as a scoop to pick up water and to fan over coals to create a flame. He slapped his horse with it to get the animal moving. His bandana—a large handkerchief worn around his neck—kept the dust out of his face in a windstorm and soaked up sweat. His chaps protected his legs. His boots had high tops to protect his legs from rattlesnakes, pointed toes to slip quickly into the stirrup, and high heels to hold his foot in place. One cowboy, W. H. Thomas, said he slept "out under the stars with a slicker for a cover, my saddle blanket for a mattress, my boots under my neck, and my saddle for a pillow."

The horse was critical to a cowboy's job, but most cowboys used a ranch's horses rather than owning their own. A cowboy depended on his horse to stand still while he roped something and to move quickly when danger was near.

▲ A saddle might last a cowboy 30 years.

A Cowboy's Saddle
A leather saddle was a cowboy's most valuable possession. It had to be comfortable, since he spent 12 to 15 hours a day sitting in it. It had a horn with a long neck so a rope could be tied around it. The wide stirrups gave him a sturdy place to stand while staying on the horse.

▲ A cowboy's hat was probably his favorite possession. He used his rope, or lariat, to catch loose cattle or horses, or to pull logs.

◄ In his saddle pack, a cowboy had a slicker—an oiled cotton coat—to put on when it rained, a blanket, and a few biscuits.

A "stock" horse was fast, agile, and had powerful back legs. It seemed to know how cattle would move and react.

A "night" horse—one with very good night vision—could see holes or loose rocks while its rider was on night watch.

A "roping" horse was trained to stand very still while the cowboy threw his rope and pulled a steer onto the ground so he could tie it up.

A cowboy used a "cutting" horse to move calmly through a herd of cattle. Cutting was the skill of moving a particular cow out of the herd.

◀ Frederic Remington's painting *Aiding a Comrade* shows a cowboy facing danger. Remington (1861–1909) based his work mainly on sketches done on his visits to the West.

Riding the line

Until the 1880s, most western ranches let their cattle wander free on the open range. The cattle found their own water and the grassy areas they liked best. Cowboys rode out constantly to check on them and the range. This was called riding the line because the cowboys rode around the line that divided neighboring ranches. Such lines were imaginary, as ranchers did not own the range but had agreed that each ranch would have a specific area of it. Cowboys did not rush when riding the line but rode calmly, keeping a count of their ranch's cattle. They tried to keep the cattle from wandering into another ranch's area. They also watched for rustlers—cowboys that were cattle thieves. During the summer, a few cowboys might move a herd to another part of the range where there was more lush grass or more water.

Saving cows

A cowboy had to watch continually for problems with the cattle. When he found cattle that were stuck in the mud or between rocks, he roped them and pulled them free. He looked for sick cattle such as those with sores. He had to treat the sores to save the animal from dying.

On the Trail

"Head 'em up. Move 'em out!"

After the spring round-up, teams of cowboys took herds of cattle from the Texas range to towns and ranches in the north. These trips took a lot of time and effort.

▲ A cowboy would use his lariat to rescue an animal trapped in mud on the riverbed.

A cattle drive was the journey in which cowboys walked their cattle from the range to where they were sold. They followed general routes, or trails. The trails that were established during the cowboy era went north to railroad towns in Kansas or to ranches in Dakota, Montana, or Wyoming. A few trails went west to Colorado. Sometimes cattle were trailed to northern ranches to graze until they weighed more and would fetch a better price at markets.

One of the first trails was the Goodnight-Loving Trail, which Charles Goodnight and Oliver Loving used in 1866 to take cattle to New Mexico and to gold mines in Colorado. In 1867, trail bosses began using the Chisholm Trail to bring cattle to Joseph McCoy's stockyards at the railroad in Abilene. The trail was named for trader Jesse Chisholm, who earlier had led wagons on the route.

► Crossing rivers could be dangerous for both cattle and cowboys. Most cowboys did not know how to swim, and cattle could be swept away in rivers fast and full from spring rains. One drover, or trail boss, would lead a drive with a herd of cattle from several ranches.

▼ A cattle drive would take two to four months to complete. For most of the time, the cowboy was on horseback.

▼ During the spring round-up, the steers that were to be sold were separated from the rest of the herd. The drive began soon after, and these animals were often combined with cattle from other ranches until thousands of cattle made up the traveling herd.

▲These cowboys from the Matador Cattle Company, Texas, photographed in about 1890, were probably telling stories or singing as they sat around a campfire.

A long trail north

In 1874, the Great Western Trail opened, but few used it because of attacks from Comanche and Kiowa. After these American Indians were forced onto reservations, cowboys used the trail to reach Dodge City, Kansas, and to trail cattle to Montana, Wyoming, and Dakota. It was used until the 1890s, when trail driving ended.

Moving up the trail

Cowboys forced a herd to walk along a trail, usually in a long line. For the first week, the cattle wanted to turn around and return home. But the cowboys moved them slowly and steadily across grasslands, rivers, deserts, and hills, and through both good weather and bad.

E. A. Houston, a lawyer living in Niobrara, Nebraska, remembered that in the 1880s, "cowboys came through here frequently with large herds of cattle longhorns from Texas—and they usually swam the cattle across the Missouri River with the cowboys on either side of the herd trying to guide them. It was dangerous work, but the cowboys did not seem to mind it."

Along each trail, cattle had to find grass and water. Cowboys liked to begin a drive in the early spring because grass was plentiful and cattle buyers were paying top dollar. Toward the end of the summer, the grass was gone and water in streams was low.

Lariat Skills

Cowboys practiced twirling a lariat to make a circle. Then they threw that circle to lasso, or capture, an animal. Cowboys were proud of their skill with the lariat and loved to tell tall tales about how they roped a big, ferocious bear or speeding jackrabbit.

Eating Dust

Dust and cattle for $30 a month

Cowboys spent months on a cattle drive keeping thousands of cattle moving. They worked as a team, with each cowboy having his own responsibilities. Each day the cowboys hoped the drive would go peacefully.

An experienced cowboy, the trail boss, led the cattle drive. He was responsible for the men and cattle and, at the trail's end, for selling the cattle. At least ten cowboys worked together as his team. The cowboys were not paid much, about $30 ($530 today) a month, for a mostly hard, boring, and sometimes dangerous job.

Named for their tasks

Each cowboy had a specific job. The "point man," an experienced cowboy, rode in front of the herd, set the pace, and pointed the way. "Swing riders" rode partway back, one on each side of the herd. "Flank riders" rode farther back. They forced ahead cattle that strayed back into the herd. The "drag rider" was usually a new cowboy who "ate dust" all day because he rode at the back of the herd. He made sure cattle were not left behind and forced slower cattle to keep up. "Cookie," often an older cowboy, drove the chuck wagon, set up camp, woke the cowboys, cooked and served breakfast and dinner, and provided first aid.

▲ A cowboy slept close to his boots, spurs, and lariat, ready for action.

Stories of Cowboy Life

Some cowboys wrote letters about their experiences. A few, such as "Teddy Blue" Abbott, wrote books about their life. Others wrote poems and songs such as this one about a cowboy's daily life:

"A cowboy's life is a weary thing,
For it's rope and brand and ride and sing;
Yes, day or night in the rain or hail,
He'll stay with his dogies [motherless calves] out on the trail."

A TEXAS COW BOY.
CHAS. A. SIRINGO.

▲ Because horses got tired from the hard work, each cowboy needed at least three fresh horses per day. One man, the "wrangler," was responsible for looking after the 50 to 150 horses needed for the drive.

16

A day on the trail

The cookie woke the cowboys very early and soon left, driving his chuck wagon. The wrangler, leading the herd of horses, left next. The cowboys ate breakfast, watered the cattle, and got them moving. On most days, they traveled slowly, about 10 miles (16 km) per day so the cattle would not lose weight. They would travel until they found camp. Cowboys ate cold biscuits and beef jerky while they rode, but when they stopped, the cookie gave them a hot meal.

At night, each cowboy took a four-hour shift guarding the herd. Two cowboys rode around the herd, preventing stampedes and watching for rustlers. Cowboys usually slept in their clothes because they never knew when they might have to rush off to stop a stampede.

▶ *An Angry Cow*—a painting by Olaf Seltzer (1877–1957), a one-time cowboy and railroad worker.

▼ The cookie set up camp near grass and water.

▲ The chuck wagon was a mobile kitchen. In it were stored all the cooking and eating equipment. A large barrel of water was attached to one side of the wagon. The word *chuck* was used locally then to mean food.

▶ For dinner, the cowboys usually ate beans, dried pork or beef stew, and biscuits or bread, and they drank lots of very strong, hot coffee. Sometimes, for a treat, the cookie served dried or canned fruit.

The Chuck Wagon

Charles Goodnight built the first chuck wagon for his 1866 trail drive. Chuck wagons were pulled by horses, oxen, or mules. They had shelves, drawers, and a hinged door that folded down into a table. Food and first-aid supplies, cowboys' bedrolls, and all their personal belongings were stored in the wagon. Every night, it was the center of the camp.

Stampede!

Riding at a dead run in the dark

No cowboy wanted to be caught in the middle of a stampede, a cattle herd's deadly mad dash to nowhere. So cowboys sang and whistled, watched for rustlers, and, when necessary, rode hard and fast to slow the herd.

Dangers stalked every cattle drive. In the early years, American Indians raided the drives to capture the horses. Cattle drives were slowed by blinding dust storms, wild prairie fires, dry watering holes, and the churning waters of flash floods. Stampedes, however, were the greatest danger on the trail. Cattle, especially Texas longhorns, were very nervous, and their huge horns were extremely dangerous. It took only a sudden, small noise or a fast movement to spook, or scare, them into blindly running in fear.

▲ Cowboys sometimes died on the trail, often trampled during a stampede. They were buried in shallow graves near the trail, and some of their grave markers can still be seen.

▼ Frederick Remington's painting *In a Stampede* showed a brave cowboy trying to control a stampede. He got the lead cattle to follow him as he turned into ever-smaller circles until they had no place to go and would stop.

▲ Cowboys wanted to be on a calm, well-trained horse when cattle took off at a run.

▲ Although any of the herd might start a stampede, the cattle would follow a lead steer if it slowed and stopped.

Calming nervous cattle

To keep the cattle calm at night, the cowboys whistled or sang as they rode night watch. It did not matter what they sang, because the steady sound of their voices calmed the cattle. But they usually sang about their loved ones or their hard lives. In 1910, John Lomax collected cowboy songs, including "The Jolly Rancher," which has this verse: "When threatening clouds do gather and herded lightnings flash, / And heavy rain drops splatter, and rolling thunders crash, / What keeps the herd from running, stampeding far and wide? / The cowboy's long, low whistle and singing by their side."

▼ At night, cattle slept on the ground. But with any sudden noise, they would get to their feet and start to panic. Cowboys would try to calm them down.

Spooked by Lightning

Cowboy "Teddy Blue" Abbott wrote of the dangers of a stampede: "If a storm came along and the cattle started running—you'd hear that low, rumbling noise along the ground and the men ... wouldn't need to come in and tell you, you'd know—then you'd jump for your horse and get out there in the lead ... before they scattered ... It was riding at a dead run in the dark, with cut banks and prairie dog holes all around you."

Cookie as a Doctor

A sick or injured cowboy relied on the cookie for medical care. But the cookie was no doctor and sometimes caused more harm than good.

Rustlers on the prowl

A cowboy wrote about his experiences with rustlers on a drive in 1879: "They [rustlers] would follow you for days ... keeping out of sight ... They would watch you as you rode around the herd on night guard ... And the whole herd would get up like one animal and light out. These rustlers ... would cut in ahead of you ... and would cut off anywhere from 50 to 200 head of big, strong, lead steers ... The fellows on night herd started shooting, and the rest of us woke up and grabbed for our horses ... they got away with the cattle."

▲ When getting ready to sleep, cowboys took great care not to make sudden noises that would frighten their animals.

▲ A cowbell might be placed on the lead steer to help find it after a stampede.

At the Railhead

The rowdy end of a trail

Once a drive reached the railroad, cowboys wanted to escape the herd of cattle, with its smell, dust, and relentless responsibility. They were anxious to clean up and enjoy themselves in town.

After two or three months on a long, dangerous, dusty trail, everyone was glad to see a town. Along the railroad, towns such as Abilene and Dodge City, Kansas, grew quickly because of cattle and cowboys. They were called cow towns. Once the trail boss had made a deal to sell the cattle, the cowboys brought the cattle to the stockyards and their duties on the drive were over.

Payday

The cowboys were smelly and tired and had been wearing the same clothes for months. As soon as they had their cash, about $30 a month for two months or more, they headed for a bath, a haircut, and new clothes. Then they went to celebrate.

▲ At the railhead, cattle were held in stockyard pens until they left on the train. Some stockyards boasted that 40 cattle cars were filled each day.

◄ Cowboys used long poles to poke and prod the cattle to move them through the stockyard pens and chutes, up the ramp, and onto waiting railroad cars. This gave the cowboys the names cowpokes or cowpunchers.

▼ The people of Dodge City, Kansas, called their home the "cowboy capital of the world" and for ten years accepted dangers such as cattle running through their streets.

Cutting loose

In 1868, 75,000 cattle were led along the Chisholm Trail to Abilene, but that grew to 700,000 in 1871. Up to 6 million Texas cattle used the Great Western Trail to Dodge City from 1875 to 1885. As the herds on the trail got bigger, so did the number of cowboys coming to town to celebrate. When cowboys headed to the saloon, they most often got drunk. Drunken cowboys did crazy things, like roping a saloon's bar and moving it outside. They gambled, but they mostly lost to the professional gamblers who came to town to win their money. When music played, they danced with anyone they could find.

A Battle for Business

As the number of herds coming up the trails grew, cattle buyers competed to purchase the cattle and railroads to ship them. Buyers rode out to meet herds or nailed posters along the trail that said they offered better deals than other buyers. The cattle went to huge stockyards in big cities such as St. Louis and Chicago.

CATTLE MEN READ THIS!

Great Inducements to those who wish to

Ship Cattle on the U. P. Railroad!!

Having entered into special arrangements with the U. P. R. R. Company, by which I can ship Cattle East at greatly reduced rates, and having selected a point between Carter and Church Buttes Stations some ten miles East of the former place, near the junction of the Big and Little Muddies, and having Constructed Commodious Lots and Extensive Enclosures, and the Company having put in a Switch capable of holding 40 Cars, I will be Prepared to Commence Shipping on or before the 15th of the Present Month, and will be able to promptly ship any Number of cattle that may be Offered.

The cattle yards are in an enclosure of some 400 acres, and stock scales and all conveniences for shipping will be furnished. If parties do not wish to ship themselves, I will purchase, at good prices, all shipping cattle that may be offered. As cattle are now bearing excellent prices East, it would be well for persons to bring their Cattle forward as soon as possible.

For further particulars, address
W. A. CARTER,
Fort Bridger, Wyo. Ter.

Fort Bridger, July 2, 1877.

Paying for damage

Cowboys went into cow towns on their days off or stayed all winter. E. F. Forsgard lived in Waco, Texas, and saw how "the cowboys would come in with herds and . . . get drunk and shoot and yell around some but nobody paid any attention to them. If they shot out any show windows in the stores, their boss man would go around to the merchants and ask them what the damage was and pay it. If the cowboys got to shooting too much, the storekeepers would put up heavy wooden shutters before the windows . . ."

▲ Most cowboys celebrated the end of the trail by spending part of their pay on gambling, drinking, and enjoying the company of ladies.

21

Guns and Rifles

Why the West was sometimes wild

Improved guns and rifles changed western life. They were used for protection and misused in many deadly ways. They made cow towns dangerous places to visit.

The new repeating rifles and six-shooters were fast and reliable. The U.S. Army used them to defeat American Indians such as the Comanche. Cowboys used them against rattlesnakes and rustlers, but the rustlers had them, too. A lot of shootings in towns were just crazy high spirits—using store signs and street lamps for target practice, for example—but cowboys did use guns against one another. It was not unusual for drunken cowboys to start a fight in a saloon. Frequently these fights ended up with guns drawn, shots fired, and deaths.

▲ ▼ Most cowboy shootouts involved one or more drunken cowboys. Cowboys wore their guns into town to impress the ladies, but most ladies were frightened by this.

Guns on the Trail

Some cowboys carried guns or rifles on the trail, but many trail bosses required the guns to be kept in the chuck wagon. The bosses were afraid guns fired by accident or in anger would injure or kill cowboys or start a stampede.

◄ Annie Oakley was possibly the best shot of all time, but she was not a cowgirl. She won shooting contests and did trick shooting. She traveled the world with Buffalo Bill's Wild West Show. Her friend, the Lakota leader Sitting Bull, called her "Little Sure Shot."

▲ The Winchester repeating rifle was known as "the gun that won the West." It could be fired rapidly and accurately.

▲ The Colt revolver was called a six-shooter because it fired six shots before it had to be reloaded.

Dodge City: the most wicked town

Founded in 1872, Dodge City, Kansas, was the last and busiest Kansas cow town. Emanuel Dubbs, one of its earliest settlers, wrote in a 1909 book that "the name of Dodge City, Kansas, was known far and wide ... The town grew almost in a night into a tented little city, every man was a law unto himself. In a few days 'Boot Hill' grave yard was started. At the approach of night the dance hall, saloons and gambling halls were a blaze of light and activity. The sharp report of the six-shooter became a nightly occurrence, and in the morning the usual question was: how many were killed last night?" Soon after it began, Dodge had 19 saloons and a gambling hall and was called one of the most wicked towns in the old West. This reputation lasted for ten years.

▶ Cowboys carried their guns in a holster, so it was easy to pull them out quickly.

Sharpshooting

Cowboys often passed the time practicing with their guns. They shot at targets such as rocks and plants. They needed to be a quick shot to kill the rattlesnakes that attacked them or to hunt for rabbits or antelope for their dinner. They held contests, sometimes against a professional shooter such as Annie Oakley.

▼ After law and order was introduced to Dodge City, gunfights broke out in only one part of town—where saloons, dance halls, and the gambling hall were allowed.

Changing the town's image

Dodge City had so many problems that the city hired Wyatt Earp to be the assistant marshal. This made many business owners unhappy, for they earned their living off the rowdy cowboys. Earp encouraged the town to divide into two parts along the railroad track. No guns were allowed on one side of the "deadline." On the other side, entertainment was provided for the cowboys.

Outlaws and Lawmen

Breaking the rules, keeping the peace

Violence and illegal activities made the West wild, but soon people began passing laws. To enforce the laws, they hired lawmen and sometimes went after outlaws on their own. Sometimes this led to more violence and deaths.

At first, people in cow towns did not enforce laws because they wanted to keep the cowboys happy. Then new settlers came with different ideas. They passed new laws and hired a lawman to "clean up" their town and enforce laws. In 1871, Abilene's new city government asked Wild Bill Hickok to be the town marshal, but those in charge soon found they did not like how he did the job. After only four years, Abilene was closed to cowboys and cattle. In 1892, Abilene businessman Charles Moreau Harger recalled in *Scribner's Magazine* "that might was the only law, and if . . . a marshal was found, like William Hickok, the original Wild Bill, who could rule an Abilene in its rudest period, it was because he was quicker with the revolver and more daring than even the cowboys themselves."

▼ Lawmen printed posters about the thieves and killers who were wanted—and the rewards given for those caught.

REWARD

$10,000

IN GOLD COIN

Will be paid by the U.S. Government for the apprehension

DEAD OR ALIVE

of

SAM and BELLE STARR

Wanted for Robbery, Murder, Treason and other acts against the peace and dignity of the U.S.

THOMAS CRAIL

▶ The county sheriff's office and jail were often in the same room. A number of outlaws escaped from jail with help from their friends.

Gunfight at the OK Corral

In 1881, near the OK Corral in Tombstone, Arizona, the Clanton gang of cowboys, rustlers, and robbers fired on Wyatt Earp, his brothers, and Doc Holiday, who represented the law. In 30 seconds, about 30 bullets flew, killing three and injuring three.

▼ Sometimes a cowboy thought he was better than a famous lawman and would challenge the lawman to a gunfight.

The bad and the good

The most common outlaws were cattle rustlers. The worst worked in outlaw gangs, stealing many cattle, robbing banks or stagecoaches, and killing people. Lawmen, such as the Texas Rangers, sheriffs, and marshals, went after them. Also, ranchers joined together into cattlemen's associations to stop rustlers. The members might ride out themselves, as vigilantes, to find the rustlers or hire men who were good with a gun to do it. Vigilantes were people who took law enforcement into their own hands. They captured and punished those people they believed were killers or cattle rustlers without paying attention to the law.

Sometimes it was hard to tell the difference between an outlaw and a lawman. Men who were good with their guns were asked to become the sheriff, even if they had shot someone in an argument in another town. In 1936, lawman Elfego Baca told an interviewer about his days in western towns and said that he "... never wanted to kill anybody ... but if a man had it in his mind to kill me, I made it my business to get him first."

▲ Legend says Billy the Kid killed 21 men, but he probably killed only four.

Fenced In, Forced Out

Dividing up the open range

Over time, the range became more crowded with farms, ranches, and cattle. Disagreements led to wars, and bad weather caused even more destruction. The cattle industry and cowboy life changed forever.

By 1890, ranchers had unofficially claimed much of the open range, while the government was selling the same land to farmers. Most cattle drives had ended because barbed-wire fences crossed trails and railroad stops were closer to ranches. Also, states had closed their borders to cattle drives, for they did not want the problems brought by cowboys or the disease and damage brought by Texas cattle.

Battles over the range

Barbed wire kept cattle off farm fields and on a ranch's grasslands. But more cattle grazed on less land, so the grass was eaten too fast and had no time to grow back. Battles broke out about land use, the causes of overgrazing, and fencing the range. Fences were cut, animals were destroyed, and people were killed.

In the late 1880s, farmer J. W. Hagerty watched barbed-wire fences going up in Texas: "Mr. Harpole had just about completed half of the fencing of his range when . . . men who were opposed to the fence organized a crew . . . the fence was destroyed . . . Harpole rebuilt the fence and [it] was guarded for about two weeks . . . it was again destroyed."

▲ Barbed wire is made of metal wire spikes stuck between twisted metal wires.

▲ A group of fence-cutters in Nebraska in 1900 disguise themselves from the photographer.

The Range Wars

In 1892, large ranchers in Johnson County, Wyoming, passed laws against small ranchers. They believed small ranchers were rustling cattle and causing overgrazing. The cattle barons hired gunmen and went after the men on their list. They attacked and burned one ranch but were trapped by 200 men at another. For two days, shots were fired. Then the governor asked for U.S. Army troops to break up the fighting and bring an end to the Johnson County War.

▲ In the Pleasant Valley Range War in Arizona in the 1880s, cattle ranchers fought with sheepherders and their supporters. Animals and people were killed.

Years of weather disasters

In the early 1880s, droughts—long periods with little or no rainfall—meant even less grass. The cattle became thin and weak. Then in 1885, blizzards hit the southern ranges. That spring, ranchers found thousands of dead cattle. Some surviving cattle were sent to the northern ranges to fatten up. The next winter, even stronger blizzards hit the northern ranches and lasted for months. Hundreds of thousands of cattle were found dead when spring finally arrived.

A changed cattle industry

Ranching and being a cowboy changed after the winter of 1886. Many ranches went out of business, and those left kept smaller herds on fenced land they owned or rented. Cowboys had to grow hay, repair windmills, and build and fix fences. A cowboy song of the time comparing the bad and good old days of the round-ups ended with the phrase (and was also titled) "The Camp-Fire Has Gone Out."

"The Great Die-up"

In the springs of 1886 and 1887, dead cattle were found packed together along barbed-wire fences as if trying to stay warm in the winter storms.

▼ During the winter the cowboys brought hay to the cattle and pulled out those trapped in the snow.

▼ When settlers built farms, they sometimes ignored the trails, so cattle wandered near their homes and trampled their fields. Farmers helped pass laws to stop the cattle drives from coming near.

▲ The Sears mail-order catalog showed the cowboys versions of items they needed, such as saddles. The cowboys sometimes papered their bunkhouse with pages from the catalog so they had something to read over the long winter.

The End of an Era
From cattle herders to movie stars

As the golden age of cowboys, cow towns, and cattle drives came to an end, the legend of the West and the people who had lived there continued to grow. The legend was fed, and still is, by new books, Wild West shows, paintings, and movies.

◄ **Children play with cowboy toys and act out legends about life in the Wild West.**

Cowboys Today

Today, cowboys have many of the same chores of the early *vaqueros*, but they herd cattle with helicopters, use electric branding irons, and move cattle in trucks. Some ranches raise goats, horses, or sheep as well as cattle. Rodeos showcase the cowboy skills of roping and riding broncos.

The trail drives and the open range ended and new technology invaded cowboys' lives. L. M. Cox, a Texas rancher in the 1880s, saw the changes. In 1937, he said, "We don't have ranches any more; just windmill and pasture projects . . . I tried for awhile to fall in with the their new-fangled ways but when they got to roundin' up and herdin' in Ford cars I thought it was about time . . . [to be] retired." Several cowboys wrote about their adventures on the range and in cow towns. This was not what Americans thought of as the West, though. Their ideas came from fictional stories that created romantic heroes, evil villains, and gunshooting marshals.

◄ **Charles Russell (1864–1926) had been a cowboy, but his paintings, such as this *Death of a Gambler* (1904), were done to entertain. They added to the legend of the West by showing its wild life.**

BUFFALO B

▼ Dime novels were inexpensive adventure books. Their stories made legends of lawmen and outlaws.

RT K. BETTS, IN OF THE GOLDEN WEST
ZONA COWBOY

▼ A cotton manufacturer used a cowboy scene to advertise the strength of its product.

"TESTING"
RK'S O.N.T. SPOOL COTTON.

ILD WEST AND CONGRESS OF ROUGHRIDERS OF THE WORLD

S OF THE COWBOY

The legend begins . . .

Starting in the 1870s, authors who had never been to the West created exciting stories about cowboys. In Wild West shows, real people from the range, like Buffalo Bill, acted out exciting incidents designed as entertainment. They made life in the West look like one big adventure. The first movie to tell a real story was a 1903 western, *The Great Train Robbery*, but it used actors and was made on the East Coast.

. . . and continues

The events in those first stories about the West became legends. A legend is a story, not necessarily based on facts, that people accept as true. The legends started with the lawmen and outlaws but often included cowboys. The legends show conflicts between an unreal, perfect hero and something or someone else, such as American Indians, ranchers, outlaws, or technology. The setting usually shows a simple life in the American West from 1866 to 1900. In these stories, the hero always wins and, in many movies, he has a wonderful singing voice. These images are now part of American culture.

▼ A big ranch was the setting for Owen Wister's 1902 novel, *The Virginian*, about the Johnson County War. It was the first to use the cowboy character as still seen in books and movies today.

▲ A modern cowboy rounding up a herd.

◄ From 1883 to 1909, Buffalo Bill's Wild West Show was action-packed entertainment. The show used real cowboys and American Indians.

29

Glossary

barbed wire twisted wire with sharp points, used for fences

brand mark burned into the hide of a cow to show who owns it, or the act of putting a brand on an animal

breed to produce young animals, particularly to get a new or improved type; a program of the mating of two breeds to create a new breed

bunkhouse building on the ranch where cowboys sleep

cattle drive long journey to walk cattle from a ranch to another place, such as another ranch or a stockyard

chaps long pieces of wool or leather worn over a cowboy's pants to protect the legs

chuck wagon wagon taken out on round-ups and cattle drives where a cook prepares meals

Civil War (1861–1865) in the United States, a war between people in northern and southern states. The South, or Confederacy, wanted to let new states have the right to own slaves. The North, or Union, did not want slavery

cow town town at the end of a cattle trail where cows were boarded onto trains

drought a shortage of rain so severe that it affects plants and the water supply

hide animal skin. Leather is made from the hide of cattle

gambling playing games for money by risking your own money

investors people who put money into a business and expect to make a lot more money in return

lariat long rope used for catching animals

marshal law officer in charge of a town

overgraze to allow grass in an area to be eaten so fast by animals, such as cattle, that it has no time to grow back

prairie area of flat or gently rolling grasslands without many trees

ranch farm where cattle, horses, or sheep are raised

range area of open land used for a particular purpose

rodeo exhibition to display cowboy skills, such as roping, often done after a round-up

round-up gathering of cattle to sort, brand, or take on a cattle drive

rustler cattle or horse thief

saloon place where alcoholic drinks are sold

sheriff law officer in charge of a county

slave someone who is owned by another person and is made to work for them

stampede sudden mad dash of cattle when they become frightened

stockyard fenced-in area where cattle are sorted and kept before being loaded onto trains or sent to slaughter houses

tallow fat from cows that is melted and used to make candles, soap, and other things

trail boss person in charge of the cattle drive

vaquero (vah-'keh-ro) in Spain and Mexico, skilled rider who took care of the cattle

windmill a tall set of blades that revolves in the wind and runs a pump that draws water from the ground

wrangler person who looks after the horses on a ranch or cattle drive

Timeline

1493 Christopher Columbus arrives in the Americas on his second voyage, bringing cattle and horses

1520 First herd of cattle brought to Mexico

1821 Mexico, including Texas, becomes independent from Spain

1836 Texas becomes a republic independent from Mexico

1845 Texas joins the United States

1846 First large cattle trail drive, from Texas to Ohio

1861–1865 American Civil War causes men to leave and cattle to remain in Texas

1862 Homestead Act offers free land in the West

1866 Charles Goodnight drives cattle to New Mexico and Colorado, beginning Goodnight-Loving Trail

1866 Charles Goodnight invents the chuck wagon

1867 Joseph McCoy builds and advertises stockyards in Abilene, Kansas

1867 The Chisholm Trail begins

1869 Transcontinental railroad completed

1871 Abilene hires Wild Bill Hickok to clean up the town and then fires him

1873 Abilene prohibits Texas cattle from entering

1874 Joseph Glidden begins selling his barbed wire

1874 The Great Western Trail opens to take cattle to Dodge City, Kansas

1875–1885 Dodge City is the biggest, wildest cow town in Kansas

1876 Railroad arrives in Fort Worth, Texas

1883 Buffalo Bill's Wild West Show begins

1884 Texas makes fence-cutting illegal

1885 Kansas and other states close their borders to Texas cattle, ending most cattle drives

1885–1887 Blizzards cause thousands of cattle to die and put many ranches out of business

1892 Large ranchers fight small ranchers in the Johnson County War in Wyoming

1900 Last herd of buffalo found in the valleys of Yellowstone, Wyoming

1902 Owen Wister publishes *The Virginian*, a novel about cowboys

1903 Release of the western movie *The Great Train Robbery*, the first that tells a real cowboy story

Information

WEBSITES

The American West
www.americanwest.com

Buffalo Bill Historical Center
www.bbhc.org

Cowboy Photographer Erwin E. Smith Collection
www.cartermuseum.org/collections/smith

Kansas Cattle Towns
www.kansascattletowns.org

Museum of the American West
http://theautry.org

National Cowboy & Western Heritage Museum
www.nationalcowboymuseum.org

The Handbook of Texas Online
See articles on "Ranching" and related topics
www.tshaonline.org/handbook

BOOKS TO READ

Freedman, Russell. *In the Days of the Vaqueros: America's First True Cowboys*. Boston: Sandpiper, 2008.

Harris, Lois. *Charlie Russell: Tale-Telling Cowboy Artist*. Gretna, LA: Pelican Publishing, 2010.

Nelson, Vaunda Micheaux, and R. Gregory Christie. *Bad News for Outlaws: The Remarkable Life of Bass Reeves, Deputy U.S. Marshal*. Minneapolis: Carolrhoda Books, 2009.

Nobleman, Marc Tyler. *Cowboy*. Chicago: Raintree, 2007.

Sheinkin, Steve, and Tim Robinson. *Which Way to the Wild West?: Everything Your Schoolbooks Didn't Tell You About America's Westward Expansion*. New York: Roaring Brook Press, 2009.

Sonneborn, Liz. *Wild Bill Hickok*. New York: Chelsea House, 2010

Index